Take back roads and backwoods
and wander on down

over roots, under branches
and vines
on the path through the brambles

and out into sun,
all ready before you—

Jubilee

Written by Ellen Yeomans

Illustrated by Tim Ladwig

Eerdmans Books for Young Readers
Grand Rapids, Michigan • Cambridge, U.K.

They'll hug and they'll holler,
they'll backslap and joke,
the old and the young and brand-new.

They'll be loud and excited,
they've waited so long
all glad to be gathered—

Jubilee

They'll have corn on the cob
and barbecue,
they'll have salt potatoes
and clams,

So much for so many
piled high as your eye,
all ready for tasting—
Jubilee

They'll have soda pop,
cold and fizzy,
and ice cream
to be churned

There'll be peaches, sweet cherries,
biscuits, pies,
and, ohhh, those berries—

Jubilee

They'll have horseshoes and hayrides
and games of all kinds—

It's kids against grown-ups
as baseballs pop-fly~

They'll have potato sack races
and wide open spaces,
all get ready, get set—
Jubilee

With shouting and singing
they'll all harmonize.
They'll warble, they'll call
and tease

They'll two-step and shuffle,
they'll clog and they'll jig,
Everyone together, little and big

swinging each other
do-si-doing around
all moving, all swaying—

Jubilee

They've saved you an ice cream.
They've saved you a dance.
They say there's room for more.

So call 'em all cousin
and come on along—
all joy is to be—

For Paige, Paddy, Ryan, Mary Elizabeth, and Jessica — all at the Jubilee
—E. Y.

To Terry C. — see you there
—T. L.

Text © 2004 by Ellen Yeomans
Illustrations © 2004 by Tim Ladwig
Published 2004 by Eerdmans Books for Young Readers
An imprint of Wm. B. Eerdmans Publishing Company
255 Jefferson S.E., Grand Rapids, Michigan 49503
P.O. Box 163, Cambridge CB3 9PU U.K.

04 05 06 07 08 09   7 6 5 4 3 2 1

Library of Congress Cataloging-in-Publication Data

Yeomans, Ellen.
Jubilee / written by Ellen Yeomans ; illustrated by Tim Ladwig.
p. cm.
Summary: Depicts a warm view of heaven as families and friends gather to celebrate the Jubilee.

ISBN 0-8028-5230-0 (hardcover : alk. paper)

[1. Heaven-Fiction.] I. Ladwig, Tim, ill. II. Title.
PZ7.Y425Ju 2003
[E]--dc21
2002151213 5-14-04

The illustrations were created with using a water color wash with liquid acrylics.
Handlettering by John Stevens
The type was set in ITC Mendoza.
Art Director Gayle Brown
Graphic Design Matthew Van Zomeren